Poems of the Heart

DAVID CONIGLIO

Half Ashe Press
Southern Pines, North Carolina 28387
halfashepress.net

ISBN: 979-8-9959376-2-3

Front cover image by David Coniglio.

For you…

Contents

Golden
Washington Song
Second Journey
Remembrance
Northampton County
Connections
Night Sounds
Unfinished Tasks
Autumn Awakening
A Dissolution of Words
Between Continents, An Ocean
Tone Poem for Two Dancers
On First Reading Sylvia Plath
Early Storm
Sumpter's Store
In the Darkest Hours
Portrait 1
Untitled #1
Northampton County Revisited
Landscape
On Cooperating with the Inevitable
Portrait 2
Taurus Moon
Untitled #2
Windows
Untitled #3
Winter Seascape
Untitled #4
Wrestling with Dragons
The Garden
For You

Golden

A dog, you said, one morning over coffee.
We should get a dog.
Young, all full of run and play and dream
this would always stay a tie that binds
us together. But dogs grow old.

In the cold of winter a season ago,
time slowed. Would that I had loved you
the way that Golden did.

Washington Song

I. Prelude

I come to you
with this gift: All I have
to give
is to lend myself to you.

II. Lament

I have done some damn fool things
in my life
but I do believe the most damn fool
one of all was the time
I got to you with sincerity.
I didn't have the guts to see you through.

III. Interlude

It starts with a darkening sky,
ever so slowly, around the edges,
like circles in the water
where a stone chanced to land,
except it happens in reverse,
from the edges in.
Ever so slowly.

Stopping it is impossible.
It moves in the bloodstream,
the nerves, the cells. A cancer
perhaps, in the non-medical sense,
but it goes to the brain just the same.
And it is contagious.

It has got me now.
Or is it the other way; I have it.
Well, that is of no consequence,
either way we have each other.
I am quite sure I got it from someone else.
Now I have passed it on to you.

I can tell. I can see it in you,
around the edges of your vision.
I know it well. I have given it to you,
even though that is not the thing I wanted,
seeing it in you. It starts with a
darkening sky.

IV. Hymn

On Sunday I watched you
asleep on the floor.
All morning you stayed curled up
in your dreams,
wrapped in that cranberry red robe,
hugging yourself.

I dreamed, awake,
of the curve of your hips,
the length of your hair, my need
to be held once more
in the cranberry red warmth
of your arms.

V. Fugue

What then,
if emptiness no longer fills.
What then?

Second Journey

You have moved away, again.
To start, again.
I move in other ways, depart
into the valley, away from sky-tipped trees,
sheltered by shadow from storm.

Should clouds break at midday
I might chance to say
I loved you. In that vow,
in waving you away, I could allow
that absolutes might do for other men.

The second journey
Is the going there again
Seeing a different view of you.

Absolutes might do for other men.

Remembrance

I never expected you
to pass this way again.
I had, on purpose, forgotten
you lived here years ago.
Those yesterdays had faded
from my mind; old joys,
joys gone sad

save for a tear now and then
in moments of deep despair
and longing for opportunities
unnoticed and long past.
I often return to walk among ruins,
reliving other lives.
I can see in the stones,

and at times in dry leaves or
dusty paths in forests deep,
other days lost to time,
to half-dreamed dreams.

I never expected you
to pass this way again,
to walk with me among the ruins.

Northampton County

When was the time you saw
wheeling, turning gulls chase home
tractor, supper hour,
row on row laid bare at autumn harvest;
cut-bone wind ocean borne,
bringing short your season?

What shut door, bright hearth
against Atlantic night led you
brow furrowed, discontent,
from familiar tomb to less known stone?
Do you not remember emptiness,
fields plowed over, late October?

Connections

I live in permanence of heart
and mind; in love
despite distance, and time,
life's fault lines.

Missed connections do not unbind
my heart from yours;
we are rejoined anew.
Homecoming.

Night Sounds

I am coming to know night sounds.
Creatures hum and click,
whirr and stir beneath my window
teaching me night sounds.

Not city sounds here, nor nature pure,
but night sounds are the sounds I hear.
Murmurs of motors measuring miles
of highway are night sounds
from highways miles away.

Thunder scores an uneven cadence
for the drumbeat of raindrops pursued
by whispers and roars of wind.
Night sounds.

I am coming to know night sounds.

Unfinished Tasks

I shall go down now and finish,
finish building the wall I planned
before you first returned;
before our time of incompleteness. Stone

to separate your land from mine; stone,
that legal owners of our lives we might remain
lest the law, too, come between us.

Stone on stone. I did not know
until you chose the wall
how I disliked unfinished tasks.

Autumn Awakening

Silver spun
web woven
enchantingly; each

thread true.
angle, arc,
pattern put

down deftly;
fibers found
dew-draped

early every
morning. Mention
then the

beauty but
watch. Waiting
quietly, quickening

hunger hastening
lethal leap,
spider strands

morning meal,
mourning mate.

A Dissolution of Words

I have come to yet another impasse.
This raw and regular retreat
to the tomb unveils the failing.

Such a dance the stance
at the face, at the face of night.
The lidded eye, the slacking mouth,

Stance calculated to recall response,
to raise the common specter of the dead.
No reply: a dissolution of words.

Between Continents, An Ocean

In the space which time fills,
the in-between time between
dream and reality.
In the space which time fills,
the space as between continents
an ocean: vast, salty, white-capped,
thundering against rock,
where land looms,
where wave and wind are wed.

That is the place to which I go
in my in-between time.
That is the place to which I go.

Tone Poem for Two Dancers

I have never seen you dance
although I have stood idly by
in time for your turns;
your over-rehearsed, well-versed
turns of phrase.

In that dark house
where I lived with you
I heard your sighs.
How you longed to confuse
ecstasy, anxiety.

Now in your season of acclaim,
I, from a different, darker house
am recalled to the night
I echoed an answering refrain.

On First Reading Sylvia Plath

Cold. Marrow-ice cold.
Branch-trunk-root solid cold.
No starburst glitters – bitter,
bitter breaking branches.

Shards skitter slicing across
stretches of snow. Oh, you.

Sylvia, do you linger in my mind
for my sake
or yours?

Where is the sense-
the sensation-
the center?

Cold. Marrow-ice cold.
Sylvia lingering.
No center.
Cold.

Early Storm

The rusted leaves flick
from the tree, wind-driven,
dancing down, down, and down.

Lost in ice and north-borne chill
branches bowed,
limbs still.

Sumpter's Store

Fan fins propellering,
propel warm winds.
Sumpter's store had hanging
only one such simple
ceiling-centered fan.

Four revolutions rounding so slowly,
marked minutes gently gliding,
wafting warmly to turn
breezes bringing lazy lamentations.
Saturday's stories.

In the Darkest Hours

Air hangs still in the darkest hours.
Sunrise waits to cut the chill of night.
I wait too, for you to rise, sleepy-eyed,
clutching the mug of coffee I placed
at your bedside just now.

Air hangs still in the darkest hours.
I rise to look outside at the waning moon
and wonder what might have been
had we not met.

There are times when you tease me:
"Sometimes you trust me too much".
Sometimes I know that might be true
in the darkest hours.

Portrait 1

Green glass and ivory beside her.
She is at the window watching,
whispering each:
the grass,
the sun,
the sky.
And she, at the window,
watching...

Untitled #1

Where can my heart go
now that it cannot go with you.
What length of days must pass
that the pulse does not quicken
to your steps and the anxious heart leap
with the sense of your presence
in the room.

Where upon earth's broad grinning face
will the memory of your sandaled feet
walk through my mind again or again
or again to haunt the night's lone hour
of slow release and tell me
at last, no more.

Where can my heart go
now that it cannot go with you.
What length of days must pass
that will erase the scorching
imprint of your hand on me.

Where upon the earth's broad
grinning face will end the searching
sadness in your eyes.

Where can my heart go
now that it cannot go with you.

Northampton County Revisited

Travel north on Route 13:
tall pines, potato fields yield
the boarded up blackened
skeleton once big-house, little-house,
quarter-house, kitchen.

What have we come to
here where terns toil
behind the tractor's disc and harrow
like poets scrabbling for words.

Landscape

When in winter
I walk along mountain ridges
I choose the trails
from forest's edge;
paths which draw against my heart
pulling deep into the wilderness.
I go alone to rediscover
the depth, the barrenness.

On Cooperating with the Inevitable

You say that if you did,
the result is you
would destroy me.

When you do not,
the result is
I destroy myself.

Either way, observe
the eventuality.

Portrait 2

I look back through yesterday
to see how brightly shined
your tears;
how thrilled the meeting
of mist and chill.

Taurus Moon

I have seen you, dreaming
the darkening pitch and roll of rain
through lightning under black-white sky,
arriving.

It is not often, in days,
I share nights' terrors; when
free in darkness
you thunder through my soul,
and out.

Untitled #2

It was time to go and she,
pausing before him, moved slightly aside
as his hand reached past her for the door.

Had others been there it would still
have passed unnoticed that he wore
the face of anguish, while her mouth
was drawn with fear that he would go.

But it was time to go, and though
they felt the force of both their wills
combined say, stay, he turned away
knowing there was no room

in either of their lives
for even so much as the touching
of one another.

Windows

From my chair by the window
the view is always the same more or less
depending on the rain or sun,
the flow of fog, or the degree of dark
in my eyes.

A front door open gives a different,
much broader view of the street;
inviting you in or asking me out
into the city.

That perhaps is why I like to go
back to my chair by the window.
The view is always the same, more or less
depending on the degree of dark
in my eyes.

Untitled #3

The words we had
neither the time
nor the courage to speak

Are the visions
which haunt us
the remainer of our days.

Winter Seascape

Demanding a share of a raging
October storm the sea has gone wild,
pounding at my feet along an endless,
aimless shore I know.

The winds, grown angry and howling
whip veils of rain and shrouds of fog flowing
over desolate miles of dunes I walk.

The roar and slap of waves on sand;
the whine, the shriek, tormenting winds
half-heard, heighten the hunger
I have for you.

When I return to lean upon the pilings,
I shall see summer seas, soft swells;
remember wind-swept sighs,
the sea and you around me.

Untitled #4

I have felt the sting of fire
that blackened your soul.
I burned for you;
with you.

The forest wild and full
with wildlife and life
gone at the casual flick of a wrist;
a twist to tear you apart,
to inhale your smoking soul.

I have felt the sting
that blackened you,
that sting of fire
I burned.

Wrestling with Dragons

Thirty years at war, my heart
waiting…waiting…waiting
for homecoming to draw near.

Wounds run deep. The salve of hope,
love's seductive whisper,
come to me, come to me here

until the dragons roar anew.
Death does not end the darkness.

The Garden

My father grew a garden in a corner of soil
behind the house in which he lived
with my mother.

Tomatoes, beans, peppers, swiss chard,
kohlrabi planted with care and tended
with love each season.

He died in the garden
one cold February day, fallen
with his rake and shovel beside him.

I love to garden, too, and when I do
I often wonder how readily the soil
receives us.

For You

You are my sun and moon,
my stars and planets and galaxies.
You are my universe.

You are my Peace of God,
past all understanding,
in heart and mind
now and forever.

www.ingramcontent.com/pod-product-compliance
Lightning Source LLC
LaVergne TN
LVHW090541110826
845146LV00003B/1212

* 9 7 9 8 9 9 5 9 3 7 6 2 3 *